Box
Stitch
CROCHET

Box
Stitch
CROCHET

Corinne
Freeman

STACKPOLE
BOOKS
Guilford, Connecticut

Published by Stackpole Books
An imprint of Globe Pequot
Trade Division of The Rowman & Littlefield Publishing Group, Inc.
4501 Forbes Boulevard, Suite 200, Lanham, Maryland 20706

Distributed by NATIONAL BOOK NETWORK
800-462-6420

British Library Cataloguing in Publication Information available
Library of Congress Cataloging-in-Publication Data

Names: Freeman, Corinne, author.
Title: Box stitch crochet : use the corner-to-corner stitch in new ways to
    make 20 hats, wraps, scarves & accessories / Corinne Freeman.
Description: First edition. | Lanham, Maryland : Stackpole Books, 2017.
Identifiers: LCCN 2017013497 (print) | LCCN 2017018534 (ebook) | ISBN
    9780811765732 (e-book) | ISBN 9780811717649 (pbk. : alk. paper)
Subjects: LCSH: Crocheting—Patterns.
Classification: LCC TT825 (ebook) | LCC TT825 .F724 2017 (print) | DDC
    746.43/4—dc23
LC record available at https://lccn.loc.gov/2017013497

First Edition

Printed in the United States of America

⊛™ The paper used in this publication meets the minimum requirements of American National Standard for Information Sciences—Permanence of Paper for Printed Library Materials, ANSI/NISO Z39.48-1992.

To my granddaughter Neavaya;
I love you more than you will ever know.

CONTENTS

Projects

Butterfly Shawl
12

Candy Stripes Cowl
16

Celebration Cuffs
& Headband   20

Latte Dream Alpaca Shrug
24

Crossing Neck Scarf
28

Down by the Bay Poncho
32

Under the Sea Motif
Shawl   36

Favorite Cowl
40

Hot Pop Neckerchief
44

Dusty Purple Motif Stole
48

Pomegranate Camisole
52

Pretty in Pink Beveled
Shawl   56

Cozy Shoulder Wrap &
Boot Toppers   60

Starlight Super Chunky
Scarf   64

Twilight Dress
68

Forest Skirt
72

Raspberry Hat & Fingerless
Gloves   76

INTRODUCTION

My interest in the box stitch started many years ago when, at a family gathering, my cousin learned this stitch from our grandmother who was blind. This dear woman loved the crochet craft, and even without her sight, she could teach my cousin. Several other family members watched in amazement as our grandmother ripped out and corrected my cousin's progress just by feeling the stitches. Later my aunt showed me the stitch; I instantly loved it, but when I asked the name of it, no one seemed to know what it was called. Sometime later I saw the stitch worked on a blog and learned the name "box stitch." But many of you may know it as the corner-to-corner stitch, or C2C.

Looking back, learning the box stitch helped me realize a confidence I may never have gained in the crochet craft. I made several million (okay, maybe a bit fewer) dishcloths using this stitch, which I gave as gifts. If I bestowed one on another crocheter, she immediately wanted to learn the stitch.

I love the texture and unique look of the box stitch. It provides a distinct definition that I have not yet found in any other stitch. Over the years, I have seen many beautiful afghans and blankets made with the stitch, but not a lot of variety of other items. Why keep this stitch in a box?! With just a little ingenuity, it can be used to create gorgeous shawls, mittens, scarves, hats, cowls, and so much more. And it is easily customizable; for sizing, I will show you how to modify a box stitch garment as you work to make it fit you just as you like.

Whether you are new to box stitch or a seasoned pro, I bet you're itching to move forward and start a project. But if you are at all unsure of the stitch, or if it is completely new to you, I urge you to look through the next chapter on techniques and practice the stitch before starting a project. It is important to note that the stitch works up diagonally and forms a triangle, which presents special considerations when creating the projects in this book. The chapter also demonstrates how to work various shapes, such as a rectangle or motif, and how to change colors while working the box stitch. Give it a look, and then begin!

The Box Stitch

Traditionally the box stitch is worked diagonally, increasing the number of boxes on each row until it is the desired width and then decreasing to make a square or rectangle. Squares and rectangles are great for blankets, which is why this stitch is often thought of as a blanket stitch. But it can be used for so much more.

First I will teach you the traditional increase and decrease for making rectangles. Then I'll show you techniques for making beveled edges and motifs and for joining so that you will be able to create the variety of shapes needed to make the designs in this book. The stitch is fairly easy and repetitive, so once you understand how it works, you'll be able to take these projects on the go and work on them without lengthy row-by-row instructions.

Box Stitch Increase

The box stitch works up into a triangle; this is the basic starting stitch:

1. Chain 6.

2. Double crochet in 4th chain from hook and in next 2 chains.

1

3. Chain 6, turn.

4. *Note:* When you turn the work to make your first double crochet in the chain 6, the first box stitch should flip from the right to the left as shown. Double crochet in 4th chain from hook and in next 2 chains. You will have 2 box stitches now.

5. Attach the first box stitch with a slip stitch to the chain-3 opening of the second box stitch.

6. Chain 3.

7. Work 3 double crochet into the same chain-3 space (there are now 3 box stitches).

- -

NOTE: The box stitch increase is worked upward in diagonal rows with the increase occurring at each end. On the third diagonal row there are some changes to the process that allow for the triangle to continue to increase and work the inside stitches of the row.

- -

8. Chain 6 to start the next increase row, turn.

9. Begin the third row of box stitches by working a double crochet in the 4th chain from the hook and in the next 2 chains.

10. Slip stitch into the chain-3 opening of the next box stitch.

11. Chain 3.

12. Double crochet 3 in the same chain-3 space.

13. Slip stitch into the chain-3 space of the next box stitch, chain 3.

14. Work 3 double crochet into the same opening.

15. Chain 6 and turn to begin the next row. Continue the process, and the box stitch will continue to increase as shown.

Box Stitch Decrease

1. When you are ready to begin a decrease row, instead of chaining 6, chain 3.

2. Turn, slip stitch into the chain-3 opening at the top of the box stitch.

3. Decrease as in step 1, then work the row as normal.

4. Work the rest of the piece to form a square. The finishing for the piece is chain 3 again, turn, and slip stitch into the chain-3 space to close the box stitch.

Rectangle

The box stitch works into a square easily. However, much of the clothing we wear requires rectangles of different sizes. You can adjust the box stitch to create rectangles of different sizes by using the increase (chain 6) on one side of the box stitch piece and the decrease (chain 3) on the other side.

- - - - - - - - - - - - - - - - -

NOTE: Some of the patterns in this book use the rectangle process but do not decrease all the way to a rectangle.

- - - - - - - - - - - - - - - - -

1. To practice this process, create a box stitch triangle with 4 box stitches across. Increase as you would normally on this side with a chain 6. This will give you a base of a 5 box stitch rectangle.

2. Work the row as normal until you reach the end. This is where you will do a decrease with a chain 3, turn, slip stitch into the chain-3 space on top of the box stitch, then work a chain 3 and 3 double crochet into the same space. Continue across the row, completing all box stitches, then increase on the other edge with a chain 6, turn.

3. Continue in this way, always increasing on the same side of the piece and decreasing on the other, until you reach the desired size of the rectangle.

4. To complete the rectangle, begin decreasing on both sides until you finish the last box stitch. In this example, the rectangle that is created has 7 box stitches on one side and 5 on the other.

Motif

By utilizing increases and decreases, you can create different shapes with the box stitch. I wanted to create pieces that looked like join-as-you-go motifs, a completely different look for the stitch.

1. For the first motif, create a square of 4 box stitches (or the desired number of stitches as indicated in the pattern). Once you reach the very last chain 3 of the square, you will work a chain 6 instead; this starts the increase process for the next motif. Double crochet in the 4th chain from the hook and in the next 2 chains. Slip stitch to join to the point of the square. Chain 6. Double crochet in the 4th chain from the hook and in the next 2 chains. Turn, slip stitch in the chain-3 space of the first box stitch, chain 3, double crochet 3 in the same chain-3 space, chain 6, turn, and continue increasing and then decreasing to make another square.

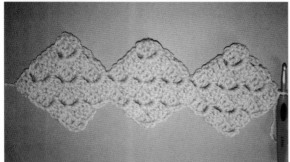

2. You will continue creating motifs to reach the length of the box stitch motif piece indicated by the pattern.

Beveled Edge

I developed the box stitch beveled edge process as a way to utilize the box stitch to create a straight piece instead of the normal diagonal. You will begin and end each piece (unless otherwise directed) with a triangle. To work the beveled edge portion, on every row you will decrease on one edge and increase on the other, balancing out each row to maintain the same number of box stitches.

1. Create a triangle 4 box stitches wide.

2. Work the decrease process at the beginning of row 5 of the triangle (chain 3, slip stitch in the chain-3 space, chain 3, double crochet 3 in the chain-3 space). Continue to work across the row as normal until you reach the 4th box stitch in this row.

Then turn your work so the chain 6 increase is at the left edge (chain 3, double crochet 3 in the chain-3 space) so that you still have 4 box stitches across this row.

3. At the end of this row, turn your work and complete another regular decrease, continue across the row until the end, and then work an increase on the left end of this row. This photo starts to show the beveled edge, with the first staggered stitch between rows 5 and 6.

4. Once the beveled edge is worked for a few rows, it will be easy to see the box stitch moving in a straight line as opposed to diagonally in a square or box.

Changing Colors

Increasing

When changing colors while increasing, finish the box stitch by working the last chain 3 and slip sttitch in the current color; this will leave two stitches. Wrap new color onto the hook and pull through the two stitches to start the new color.

Decreasing

When changing colors while decreasing, finish off the chain 3 of the box stitch. Work the slip stitch to finish the box, and with 2 loops on the hook, pull through the new color.

Joining

Because of the unique edgings on the sides of a box stitch piece, it can be challenging to sew together two pieces. I created this connecting stitch because I wanted a clean look to join box stitch pieces without having to single crochet around each piece and then sew.

Box Stitch Join

When you look at a box stitch piece, you will notice that it has two different edgings. Two sides have chain-3 spaces and 2 sides are closed. The edging with chain-3 spaces is great for adding embellishments like shell stitches, while the closed edges are best for joining.

1. Lay the two pieces so the closed edges are next to each other. Holding the two pieces together, attach the yarn at the bottom between 2 matching box stitches and knot so the yarn is secure.

2. Fold the pieces with the closed sides together, then pull the yarn through in a single crochet.

Chain 3 and secure with a single crochet between the next 2 matching box stitch edges. Continue working single crochet and chain 3 until you reach the end of the closure required.

3. Once completed, you can open up the pieces to see the join. This join is hidden in the inside part of the finished piece.

4. Flip the piece over to see the side of the join on the closed edges of the finished piece. This join is invisible when you use the same color yarn, but for these pictures I used a contrasting color so you could see the stitches.

Lattice Join

This connection is what I like to use when a piece needs a bit more flexibility. For instance, I use this closure for the Celebration Cuffs on page 22 in this book so that you can place your thumb into any of the closure stitches.

To work this join, place the closed edges together. Attach the yarn at one end of the piece and then single crochet and chain 3 in between each box stitch as shown, moving up diagonally in a lattice stitch to connect the two pieces.

PROJECTS

Butterfly Shawl

This design was my first for this book, and I named it after my granddaughter, who my husband and I refer to as our "little butterfly." I can easily imagine her in this shawl when she gets a little older.

YARN

Cascade Yarns Ultra Pima Fine (#2 fine weight; 100% pima cotton; 136.5 yd./125 m; 1.75 oz./50 g)
    4 skeins #3779 Pansy

HOOK

U.S. size G-6 (4 mm) crochet hook

GAUGE

3 x 3 box stitches = 1¾ x 2¼ in./4.5 x 5.7 cm
Note: Gauge is not critical for this project. Measure as you work to reach the desired size.

FINISHED MEASUREMENTS

33 x 51 x 33 in./84 x 130 x 84 cm, including the wings

NOTES

- This design uses the Box Stitch Increase (page 1), Decrease (page 4), and Rectangle (page 5).
- For this piece, you will be making 1 main box stitch triangle and 2 wing box stitch rectangle strips, then joining them to finish the piece. The butterfly wing effect is created by leaving the two diagonal ends of the rectangle pieces unjoined.

Instructions

Triangle

First, create the main box stitch triangle by using the box stitch increase process until you have 40 rows of box stitches. The approximate measurements of the triangle are 30 x 48 x 30 in./76.2 x 122 x 76.2 cm. Do not finish off.

Figure 1

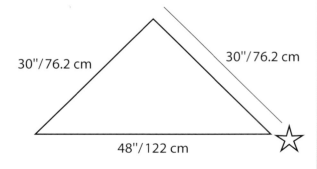

30"/76.2 cm

30"/76.2 cm

48"/122 cm

TRIANGLE EDGING

You will now create the two-row edging on the two shorter 30 in./76.2 cm sides as described. Turn the triangle so that you will be working the first side. You will be at the star as pictured in Figure 1.

Row 1: Join yarn, chain 5, work a single crochet between next 2 box stitches, continue working down the triangle in the same manner to the point of the triangle, work single crochet, chain 5, single crochet into the point. Continue to work the chain 5, single crochet to the end of the next short side of the triangle, turn.

Row 2: Chain 5, work single crochet into the first chain 5 worked on Row 1, continue until the point of the triangle and work single crochet, chain 5, and single crochet in the point. Finish this row by continuing on the other side of the triangle using the same chain 5, single crochet process.

I recommend weaving in ends and finishing off the triangle at this point.

Wing Rectangles

The next step is to create the 2 rectangle box stitch pieces that are 5 box stitches wide. You will be leaving the rectangles unfinished on one end to give the shawl the wing effect.

Work each rectangle until the longer edge is 48 box stitches and the shorter edge (at the star in the diagram) is 44 box stitches. *Note:* Because of the nature of the box stitch, you are always working on a diagonal, so this uneven end will occur naturally if you do not decrease.

WING EDGING

On each rectangle, work the chain 5, single crochet edging as you did for the triangle on the inside of the rectangle only. Each piece should have two rows of edging.

I recommend weaving in ends and finishing off the rectangles before the next step to join to the main box stitch triangle.

Joining

Working with one rectangle wing at a time, join the piece by attaching the yarn to the point of the triangle in the chain-5 space (see Figure 2; join at star); then work chain 5 and single crochet into the corresponding wing chain-5 space. Continue the chain 5, single crochet until you reach the end of the 30 in./76.2 cm triangle and wing. Repeat the process on the other side of the triangle/wing to join the pieces.

Figure 2

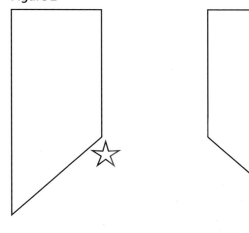

Finishing

Weave in ends and block to finish.

Candy Stripes Cowl

The cowl is created by crocheting stripes with alternating colors in cream and purple. The interest is created by varying the pattern of the stripe colors in a 5-3-3-5 color pattern repeat.

YARN

Lion Brand LB Collection Superwash Merino (#3 light weight; 100% merino wool; 306 yd./280 m; 3.5 oz./100 g)
   3 skeins #098 Ivory (Main Color, abbreviated MC)
   3 skeins #146 Wisteria (Contrasting Color, abbreviated CC)

HOOK

U.S. size G-6 (4 mm) crochet hook

GAUGE

3 x 3 box stitches = 1¾ x 1¾ in./4.5 x 4.5 cm
Note: Gauge is not critical for this project. Measure as you work to reach the desired length before joining.

FINISHED MEASUREMENTS

Circumference: 34 in./86.4 cm
Height with edgings: 10 in./25.4 cm

NOTES

• This design uses the Box Stitch Increase (page 1), Decrease (page 4), Rectangle (page 5), Changing Colors Increasing and Decreasing (page 8), and Box Stitch Join (page 9).

STITCH GUIDE

Beginning Shell = chain 3 and 4 double crochet
Shell = 5 double crochet

Instructions

Rectangles

Create 2 identical box stitch rectangles as follows: Starting with MC, work 5 rows of box stitch increase;

the piece will be 5 box stitches wide. Change to CC and work 3 rows, continuing to use the increase box stitch. You should now have 8 rows consisting of 5 MC and 3 CC. Switch to MC and work row 9; at the end of row 9, work the decrease box stitch to begin creating the rectangle. Continue decreasing on one side of the strip and increasing on the other, working the color pattern of 5 rows MC, 3 rows CC, 3 rows MC, 5 rows CC. Work each strip until it is approximately 34 in./86 cm in length, then decrease on both sides to finish the rectangle.

Joining

Once the desired length is reached in each rectangle, join the two strips lengthwise with MC and the box stitch join. Match up each stripe so that the pieces align and make the pattern as shown in the picture. Next fold the piece in half and join the edges to create the cowl.

Edging

Round 1: Connect MC to any opening between 2 box stitches, chain 6 (counts as a double crochet and chain 3), work 1 double crochet in between next 2 box stitches, continue with chain 3 and 1 double crochet between box stitches until you have completed the round. Join round with a slip stitch into chain 3 of the beginning chain 6.

Round 2: Connect CC into any chain-3 space of the previous round, chain 6 (counts as a double crochet and chain 3), in the next chain-3 space work 5 double crochets to create a shell, chain 3 and dc into the next chain-3 space. Continue round by chain 3, dc into next chain 3 and then chain 3 and create 5 dc shell into the next chain-3 opening. Finish round by joining with a slip stitch into the 3rd chain of the beginning chain 6.

Round 3: Connect MC into any chain-3 space between a double crochet and shell. Work beginning shell into chain-3 opening, slip stitch into the 3rd dc of previous row's shell, then work two 5 dc shells on either side of the dc stitch. Finish with a slip stitch to beg shell or round.

Finishing

Weave in ends and block to finish.

Celebration Cuffs & Headband

During an early spring or late fall festival, the wind can create just enough of a chill to warrant cozy accessories. I created the Celebration Cuffs & Headband to not only provide that bit of warmth but to stand out as special and fun, worthy of a celebration!

YARN

SweetGeorgia Yarns Cashluxe Spark (#1 super fine; 80% superwash merino, 10% cashmere, 10% spark; 420 yd./384 m; 4 oz./115 g)
   1 skein Cherry

HOOK

U.S. size H-8 (5 mm) crochet hook
1 button (¾ in./2 cm)

GAUGE

3 x 3 box stitches = 2 x 2 in./5 x 5 cm

FINISHED MEASUREMENTS

Headband: Length 23 in./58 cm; width 6 in./15 cm; circumference 8½ in./22 cm (this can change depending on button placement)
Cuff: Length 6 in./15 cm; width 3½ in./9 cm; circumference 7 in./18 cm

NOTES

- The Celebration Cuffs & Headband use the Box Stitch Increase (page 1), Decrease (page 4), Rectangle (page 5), Lattice Join (page 10, cuffs only), and Beveled Edge (page 7, headband only).

Cuffs

I like options, and I think others do too, so I design with versatility in mind.
By using the lattice join, the thumb opening can be anywhere along the join, which
allows you to decide how much of your hand you want covered by the cuff.

Instructions

Create a box stitch rectangle 11 box stitches wide (approximately 6 in./15 cm), then work the rectangle until the cuff is 9 box stitches long. Decrease on both sides to complete the rectangle; do not finish off.

Finishing

Fold the rectangle in half to create a tube. Work the lattice join to connect the cuffs.

Headband

The fit of this headband can be adjusted to different head sizes by either increasing more of the box stitch or simply using another box stitch opening as a buttonhole, as each box stitch can be used as a buttonhole.

Instructions

Create a box stitch triangle 6 box stitches wide (approximately 7½ in./19 cm diagonally), then use the box stitch beveled edge process until you have a strip approximately 12 in./30.5 cm long. Work the regular box stitch decrease to finish off the piece.

Finishing

Weave in the ends and sew a button in the middle of one of the triangle ends. Push the button through one of the box stitch openings to close.

Latte Dream Alpaca Shrug

This piece really makes a statement, but it is one of the most straightforward patterns I've ever written. Using the box stitch adds a texture that makes it look more complicated than it is.

YARN
A to Z Alpacas Sock Weight Yarn (#2 fine weight; 100% alpaca; 718 yd./657 m; 7 oz./200 g)
> 2 skeins Latte

HOOK
U.S. size G-6 (4 mm) crochet hook

GAUGE
3 x 3 box stitches = 1¾ x 1¾ in./4.5 x 4.5 cm

FINISHED MEASUREMENTS
Rectangle before folding: 28 x 36 in./71 x 91.5 cm

NOTES
- This design uses the Box Stitch Increase (page 1), Decrease (page 4), Rectangle (page 5), and Box Stitch Join (page 9).

Instructions

Create a box stitch rectangle 48 x 66 box stitches, approximately 28 x 36 in./71 x 91.5 cm.

Armholes

Create the armholes by folding the longest side in half and then use the box stitch join on both sides for approximately 9 in./22.8 cm. This can be adjusted as required depending on the size needed for the arms.

36"/91.5 cm

28"/71 cm

Fold here

18"/45.7 cm in total

28"/71 cm

9"/22.8 cm connected

Arm openings

Crossing Neck Scarf

You can wear this scarf with a shawl pin to join it or wrap it around your neck for extra warmth. To create the mirror-image staggered scarf ends, you will create 2 box stitch pieces that will be joined at the back.

YARN

SweetGeorgia Yarns Superwash Worsted (#4 medium weight; 100% superwash merino wool; 200 yd./182 m; 4 oz./115 g)
   1 skein Slate

HOOK

U.S. size M/N-13 (9 mm) crochet hook

GAUGE

3 x 3 box stitches = 2½ x 2½ in./6.4 x 6.4 cm
Note: Gauge is not critical for this project. Measure as you work to the desired length before joning.

FINISHED MEASUREMENTS

6 x 58 in./15.25 x 146 cm

NOTES

• This design uses the Box Stitch Increase (page 1), Decrease (page 4), Rectangle (page 5), and Box Stitch Join (page 9).

Instructions

Scarf Ends

Create 2 box stitch rectangles, as follows: Work box stitch increase until the piece is 8 box stitches wide (approximately 6 in./15.25 cm). Continue to work the piece as a rectangle (decreasing on one side only) until it is 27 box stitches (approximately 25 in./63.5 cm) on the short edge and 34 box stitches on the long edge (approximately 29 in./73.5 cm). Do not decrease to complete the rectangle; leave the edges uneven as shown in the photos.

Join Ends

Use the box stitch join to secure the two pieces so the opposite sides of the unfinished rectangles are away from each other. The seam should be on the underside of the joined pieces so it isn't seen when worn (see Figure 3).

Finishing

Weave in ends and secure with a shawl pin or a button if desired.

Figure 3

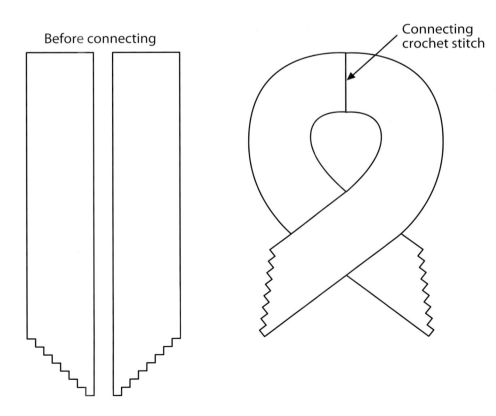

Before connecting

Connecting crochet stitch

Down by the Bay Poncho

I love ponchos and find it very exciting that they are often in style. This particular poncho turned out beautifully with this yarn from Interlacements. The drape, color, and style are just perfect.

YARN

Interlacements Yarns Rick Rack (#2 fine weight; 100% rayon; 1,200 yd./1,097 m; 16 oz./454 g)
    1 skein Sturgeon Bay

HOOK

U.S. size H-8 (5 mm) crochet hook

GAUGE

3 x 3 box stitches = 2 x 2 in./5 x 5 cm

FINISHED MEASUREMENTS

Gathered neckline: 46 in./117 cm
Middle neckline to bottom of box stitch triangle: 30 in./76 cm
Arm length: 16 in./38 cm

NOTES

- This design uses the Box Stitch Increase (page 1), Decrease (page 4), and Box Stitch Join (page 9).

Instructions

Create two identical box stitch triangles, as follows:
Work the box stitch increase until you reach 34
box stitches across the widest part of the triangle
(approximately 36 in./91 cm). Then work the box
stitch decrease until you reach 15 box stitches. You
will be leaving these stitches unworked to create the
staggered neckline.

Finishing

Weave in the ends and use the box stitch join for
the first three (or more if desired) box stitches
together on each side of the neckline to create the
shoulder/arm closure. You can add more joining
stitches, if you like, or use buttons at the shoulders.
To create armholes, use joining from waist up to
create desired openings.

Figure 4

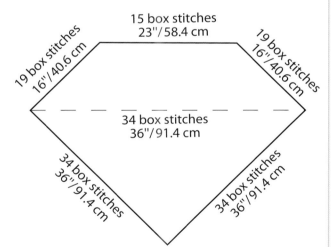

15 box stitches
23"/58.4 cm

19 box stitches
16"/40.6 cm

19 box stitches
16"/40.6 cm

34 box stitches
36"/91.4 cm

34 box stitches
36"/91.4 cm

34 box stitches
36"/91.4 cm

Under the Sea Motif Shawl

I have not seen the box stitch used as a crochet motif, but I love the look of motifs in afghans, blankets, and stylish clothing. I wanted to create a look that would utilize the box stitch motif process but also have other harmonious elements. You will be working three separate motif rows and an outlining border in the same color. Wear this piece as a warm, casual stole or as a chunky scarf.

YARN

Red Heart Unforgettable (#4 worsted weight; 100% acrylic;
270 yd./247 m; 3.5 oz./100 g)
    7 skeins Dragonfly

HOOK

U.S. size G-6 (4 mm) crochet hook

GAUGE

3 x 3 box stitches = 1¾ x 1¾ in./4.5 x 4.5 cm
Gauge of the 15 box stitch motif is approximately
9½ x 9½ in./24 x 24 cm.

FINISHED MEASUREMENTS

47 x 28 in./120 x 72 cm

NOTES

- This design uses the Box Stitch Increase (page 1), Decrease (page 4), Motif (page 6), and Lattice Join (page 10).
- See diagram for motif layout.

Instructions

Motif Rows

For this pattern you will construct three rows of the box stitch motif that are 15 box stitches square. A box stitch motif is a box stitch square; you will use the box stitch increase and decrease to create each motif. The connection between each motif is worked by decreasing to the last stitch, and instead of finishing the square by doing the chain 3, you start the increase again with the chain 6 and start a new box stitch motif. Two of the motif rows have 4 box stitch motifs, and the other has 5 box stitch motifs. After each box stitch motif row is completed, create an edging by doing a chain 5 then sc around the piece 2 times. This finishing will be used in the final joining of the 3 motif rows.

Edging

Once you have finished making two rows of 4 box stitch motifs and one row of 5 box stitch motifs, the next step is to create the edging around each row. For the first edging row, join yarn between any 2 box stitches of one of the box stitch motifs, chain 5 and single crochet between each box stitch around the entire piece, and join with a slip stitch.

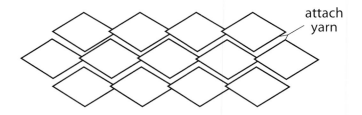

attach
yarn

For the second edging row, join yarn to any chain-5 space, chain 5 and work a single crochet in the previous row's chain 5 around, and slip stitch to the beginning chain 5.

Joining

The last step is to connect the 3 box stitch motif rows. You will join the 3 rows with the longest row in the middle by using the lattice close. I recommend laying out the 3 rows on a flat work space to align for the box stitch lattice closure.

Attach the yarn at the end of a row into one of the chain-5 spaces. Chain 2, then single crochet into the opposite chain-5 space on the other row of the box stitch piece; continue until the end of the 2 pieces.

Repeat to join the other 4-motif row to the middle 5-motif row.

Finishing

Weave in the ends and block. This piece requires blocking to lie flat and look its best.

Favorite Cowl

You will want to wear this cowl every day. Dress it up, dress it down—it makes every outfit special. If you prefer a scarf, just omit the join.

YARN

Berroco Artisan (#4 medium weight; 80% merino wool, 20% silk; 123 yd./112 m; 1.75 oz./50 g)
    2 skeins #6007 Gulf of Maine

HOOK

U.S. size M/N-13 (9 mm) crochet hook

GAUGE

3 x 3 box stitches = 3 x 3 in./7.6 x 7.6 cm
Note: Gauge is not critical to this project. Measure as you work to reach the desired size.

FINISHED MEASUREMENTS

4½ x 68 in./11.5 x 173 cm

NOTES

- This design uses the Box Stitch Increase (page 1), Decrease (page 4), Rectangle (page 5), and Box Stitch Join (page 9).

Instructions

Work the box stitch increase until your piece is 5 box stitches wide (approximately 4½ in./11.5 cm). Then work in a rectangle (decreasing on one side only) until the piece is 60 box stitches long (approximately 68 in./173 cm), then decrease on both edges to finish the rectangle.

Finishing

Join the two 5-box-stitch-wide ends together to create the infinity scarf. Weave in the ends and block if necessary.

Hot Pop Neckerchief

Wear this accessory three different ways: tied in front as a cowl, off to the side as a scarf, or to the back. Whichever way you choose, the hot pink will draw all eyes on you.

YARN

Caron Simply Soft Party (#4 medium weight; 99% acrylic, 1% polyester; 164 yd./150 m; 3 oz./85 g)
    4 skeins Fuchsia Sparkle

HOOK

U.S. size J-10 (6 mm) crochet hook

GAUGE

3 x 3 box stitches = 2½ x 2½ in./6.4 x 6.4 cm
Note: Gauge is not critical for this project. Measure as you work to desired size.

FINISHED MEASUREMENTS with ties

35 in./88.9 cm across top
21 in./53 cm on side of triangles

NOTES

- This design uses the Box Stitch Increase (page 1).
- For a refresher on the Triple Treble Crochet, see Crochet Stitch Review on page 83.

Instructions

Triangle and Edging

Work a box stitch triangle 20 box stitches wide that is approximately 21 x 28 x 21 in./53 x 71 x 53 cm. Once this size is reached, turn the piece and in each of the chain-3 openings going down the first 21-in./53-cm side, work the following group of stitches: half double crochet, double crochet, triple treble crochet, double crochet, half double crochet. Once the peak of the triangle is reached, work the same sequence of stitches into the very top double crochet in the box stitch. Continue to create the decorative edging up the other side of the triangle; do not finish off.

Ties

The ties at the top edges are created as follows: Take the yarn that was left unfinished from the triangle, chain 20, turn, and single crochet back over the same 20 stitches. You will now work across the top of the triangle by working 1 single crochet into the top of the diagonal box stitch and then 2 single crochet in between the next diagonal box stitch, continue across to the opposite corner, chain 20, turn, single crochet back over the 20 chains, and then slip stitch into the last single crochet of the triangle.

Finishing

Weave in the ends and block.

Dusty Purple Motif Stole

This piece is a unique stole, created by making two 15-motif rows and then outlining and connecting them with black crochet yarn. It can be worn as a scarf or a stole, depending on your style of the day.

YARN

Darn Good Yarn Viscose (#3 light weight; 100% rayon/viscose; 200 yd./183 m; 3.5 oz./100 g)

    4 skeins Purple

Red Heart Fashion Crochet Thread Size 3 (#1 super fine weight; 100% mercerized cotton; 125 yd./114 m; 2.1oz./60 g)

    3 skeins Black

HOOK

U.S. size H-8 (5 mm) crochet hook

GAUGE

Gauge of each motif square (6 x 6 box stitches) = 3½ x 3½ in./ 8.9 x 8.9 cm

FINISHED MEASUREMENTS

11 x 70 in./28 x 178 cm

NOTES

- This design uses the Box Stitch Increase (page 1), Decrease (page 4), and Motif (page 6).

Instructions

Make two box stitch motif rows that are each 15 motifs long. Each motif will be 6 box stitches square, using the increase and decrease to create the motif. To end one motif and begin the next, decrease to the last stitch and instead of making the last 3 chains, chain 6 and start a new box stitch motif.

Edging

Outline each motif row with the black crochet thread by securing the thread between 2 box stitches and chaining 6 (counts as first chain 3 and double crochet). Continue outlining the motifs by chaining 3 and working a double crochet between each of the box stitches, until you reach a corner of a motif. The corners of each motif square should have 1 double crochet, 3 chains, 1 double crochet in each (this is used later on to join the two strips). Work around the entire strip, then slip stitch to join to the beginning chain 3.

Joining

Once both pieces are outlined, place the two strips side by side. You will connect the pieces at the corners of the motifs, connecting through the chain-3 spaces. Secure the purple yarn to one of the corners, then single crochet between the two corners. Chain 25, single crochet to join through

the chain-3 spaces of the next corners, and then continue chaining 25 and joining with single crochet between each motif. Take special care not to twist the motifs as you join.

Finishing

Weave in the ends and block the entire piece.

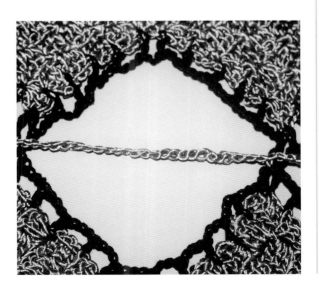

Pomegranate Camisole

The sizing on this top is easy to customize. Base the width on your bust or hip circumference, whichever is larger. You can adjust this as well by adding or subtracting box stitches, as I describe in the instructions.

YARN

Red Heart Unforgettable (#4 worsted weight; 100% acrylic; 270 yd./247 m; 3.5 oz./100 g)
  6 skeins Winery

HOOK

US G-6 (4 mm) crochet hook

GAUGE

3 x 3 box stitches = 1¾ x 1¾ in./4.5 x 4.5 cm

FINISHED MEASUREMENTS

Adjust to size desired by adding or subtracting box stitches from your main rectangle as described in the pattern.

NOTES

● This design uses the Box Stitch Increase (page 1), Decrease (page 4), Rectangle (page 5), and Box Stitch Join (page 9).

BOX STITCH SIZING—CAMISOLE

	extra sm	sm	med	large	1X	2X	3X	4X	5X
Circumference	31 in./ 79 cm	35 in./ 89 cm	38 in./ 97 cm	42 in./ 106 cm	46 in./ 117 cm	50 in./ 127 cm	54 in./ 137 cm	58 in./ 147 cm	62 in./ 158 cm
Bust to Hip (number of box stitches)	37	37	38	39	40	41	41	42	43
Circumference (number of box stitches)	54	60	67	74	81	88	95	102	109

Instructions

First, make a box stitch rectangle to your size requirements following the chart on page 53. To make the piece longer or shorter, add or subtract from the 36 box stitches; to make the top larger or smaller around, add or subtract from the 56 box stitches, keeping in mind the gauge, which is 3 x 3 box stitches = 1¾ x 1¾ in./4.5 x 4.5 cm. Try the piece on for fit before fastening off.

Straps

Make two straps as follows: Work the box stitch increase until your piece is 3 box stiches wide, then work a rectangle until it is 24 box stitches in length (or desired length to fit from the top of the bust over the shoulder to the top of the underarm in back; measure for fit and adjust the number of box stitches accordingly).

Joining

Attach the straps with the box stitch join, making sure your placement is equivalent for both the front and back straps. On the sample, the front straps were connected 5 box stitches in from the opening of the piece (or approximately 3¼ in./8.25 cm); for the back of the garment the straps were 13 box stitches apart (approximately 8 in./20.3 cm).

Finishing

To close the front of the garment over the bust, chain 312 and weave the chain through the box stitch openings lattice-style, pull, and tie closed. You could also connect it with the box stitch join or buttons.

Weave in the ends and block.

Pretty in Pink Beveled Shawl

By working the beveled box stitch, you end up with a unique and beautiful edging without the extra "edging" step. It is surprisingly simple to do, but the resulting shawl looks anything but simple!

YARN

Cascade Yarns Venezia Sport (#2 fine weight; 70% merino wool, 30% silk; 307.5 yd./281 m; 3.5 oz./100 g)

   3 skeins #193 Power Pink

HOOK

U.S. size I-9 (5.5 mm) crochet hook

GAUGE

3 x 3 box stitches = 2 x 2 in./5 x 5 cm

Note: Gauge is not critical for this project. Measure as you work to desired size.

FINISHED MEASUREMENTS

17 x 51 in./43.2 x 129.5 cm

NOTES

- This design uses the Box Stitch Increase (page 1), Decrease (page 4), and Beveled Edge (page 7).

Instructions

Start by creating a box stitch triangle that is 16 box stitches wide (approximately 15½ in./39.3 cm). Then use the beveled edge box stitch technique until the shawl is desired length minus the end triangles. Once the length is reached, you will have a shawl that has a triangle on each end and a built-in beveled edging down each side.

Finishing

Finish the shawl by weaving in the ends and blocking.

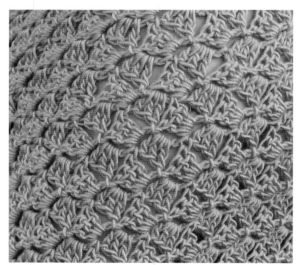

Cozy Shoulder Wrap & Boot Toppers

A dear customer inspired the idea for this warm shoulder covering. It is perfect for those chilly days and nights when you need something to cover just your shoulders. The boot toppers add extra style and warmth too.

YARN
Red Heart Comfort Chunky (#5 bulky weight; 100% acrylic; 448 yd./410 m; 12.7 oz./360 g)
> 2 skeins Cream

HOOK
U.S. size M/N-13 (9 mm) crochet hook

GAUGE
3 x 3 box stitches = 3¾ x 4 in./9.5 x 10.2 cm

FINISHED MEASUREMENTS
Sample shoulder wrap: Circumference 43 in./109 cm
Sample boot cuffs: 8½ x 14 in./22 x 36 cm
Note: Size can be easily customized by adding or subtracting box stitches; see instructions in the pattern for adjusting the size.

NOTES
- These designs use the Box Stitch Increase (page 1), Decrease (page 4), Rectangle (page 5), and Box Stitch Join (page 9).

Shoulder Wrap

Instructions

First, measure around your shoulders, above your breastbone, then subtract 1 in./2.5 cm to find the circumference you need for your wrap.

Work the box stitch increase until you have 10 box stitches in the row. This will make a wrap that is approximately 12 in./30.5 cm tall; adjust this number if you want your wrap shorter or taller. Then work a rectangle until the piece is 35 box stitches long. This will make a wrap approximately 43 in./109 cm in circumference; adjust the number of box stitches if necessary to match the circumference you determined from your measurements and gauge.

Joining

Close the wrap by joining the two shorter ends with the box stitch join.

Finishing

If desired, create a long chain and weave it into the top side of the piece to pull it tighter.

Weave in the ends and block.

BOX STITCH SIZING—SHOULDER WRAP									
	extra sm	sm	med	large	1X	2X	3X	4X	5X
Circumference	40.5 in./ 103 cm	43 in./ 109 cm	46 in./ 117 cm	49 in./ 124 cm	51 in./ 130 cm	54 in./ 137 cm	60 in./ 152 cm	64 in./ 163 cm	68 in./ 173 cm
Circumference (number of Box Stitches)	33	35	37	39	41	43	48	51	55
Length (number of Box Stitches)	9	10	11	12	12	13	13	14	14

Boot Toppers

Instructions

First, measure loosely around your mid-calf; this is the circumference for your boot cuffs.

Make two box stitch rectangle pieces that are 7 by 10 box stitches (approximately 8½ x 14 in./22 x 36 cm) or desired measurements.

Joining

Fold each cuff in half, the short closed edges together, and use the box stitch join to create the tube; do not finish off.

Edging

You will now work in rounds to provide the boot toppers with a smaller top piece that will help secure them.

Round 1: Join yarn between 2 box stitches, chain 2, then work 3 single crochet into each chain-3 opening of the box stitches around, and then slip stitch to join to the beginning chain 2; do not finish off.

Round 2: Chain 2 and then single crochet into each stitch from previous row.

Finishing

If desired, create a long chain to weave into the box stitch openings at the top or bottom to help keep the boot toppers securely above the boot.

Weave in the ends.

Starlight Super Chunky Scarf

In many parts of the world it can get very cold in the cooler months. When the temperature dips below freezing, you will love having the Starlight Super Chunky Scarf to keep you warm and cozy. The size of this piece is easily adjusted by changing the number of box stitches in the width or length.

YARN

Red Heart Stellar (#5 bulky weight; 99% acrylic, 1% other fibers; 160 yd./146 m; 8 oz./226 g)
>   5 skeins Nova

HOOK

U.S. size N (10 mm) crochet hook

GAUGE

3 x 3 box stitches = 5 x 5⅓ in./12.7 x 13.5 cm
Note: Gauge is not critical for this project. Measure as you work to reach the desired size.

FINISHED MEASUREMENTS

12 x 80 in./30.5 x 203.2 cm

NOTES

- This design uses the Box Stitch Increase (page 1), Decrease (page 4), Rectangle (page 5), and Box Stitch Join (page 9).

Instructions

Create a box stitch rectangle that is 6 box stitches wide by 45 box stitches long (approximately 12 x 80 in./31 x 203 cm). To make this into the popular infinity scarf, use the joining technique described on page 9.

Finishing

Weave in the ends and block if necessary.

Twilight Dress

I find that sometimes when I design, I start out with an idea in my head but then the creative process takes over and the intended look becomes something else. For this design, I thought I would make a long skirt with this beautiful yarn. However, once I tried it on my mannequin, I quickly realized this piece was meant to be a dress.

YARN
Blue Heron Yarns Organic Cotton (#3 light weight; 100% organic cotton; 630 yd./576 m; 8 oz./227 g)
> 2 skeins Water Hyacinth

Red Heart Fashion Crochet Thread Size 3 (#1 super fine weight; 100% mercerized cotton; 125 yd./114 m per skein; 2.1oz./60 g)
> 2 skeins Black

HOOK
U.S. size G-6 (4 mm) crochet hook

GAUGE
3 x 3 box stitches = 2¼ x 2¼ in./5.7 x 5.7 cm

FINISHED MEASUREMENTS
Sample is 33 x 43 in./84 x 109 cm. Adjust the number of box stitches as described in the pattern to create the desired size.

NOTES
- This design uses the Box Stitch Increase (page 1), Decrease (page 4), and Rectangle (page 5).

Instructions

Body

First, find the largest measurement on your body, usually the bust or hips; this will be the circumference of your dress. Create a box stitch rectangle that is 47 box stitches by 56 box stitches (approximately 33 x 43 in./84 x 109 cm) or your desired circumference and length.

Edging and Bodice

Attach the black thread to the corner of one side of the rectangle and work down the longer side as follows: chain 2, then work 3 single crochet into each of the chain-3 openings. Once the end of this edge is worked, turn, chain 2, and single crochet in each of the stitches going up along the same edge until you reach where you joined the black thread initially.

Chain 2, work 3 single crochet into each chain-3 opening along the shorter width of the piece (this will become the top of the dress).

At the next corner, chain 2, work 3 single crochet in each of the chain-3 openings down the other long side of the rectangle. At the corner, turn, chain 2, and work a single crochet into each of the single crochets going up to the top corner of the dress again. The edging going down the dress is now complete.

Once you are at the top of the piece again, turn, chain 2, work a single crochet into each single crochet across, and continue for approximately 10 rows (3 in./7.6 cm). This creates the top of the dress bodice.

Closing

The back of the dress can be closed with a chain tie, buttons, hooks, or the like. I chose to create a chain of 500, which I wove through the natural openings of the single crochet stitches in a lattice method and pulled and tied to close. You would not want to join the dress closed, as it would be too difficult to get on and off.

Forest Skirt

This skirt in this color is perfect for the first crisp days of fall. Wear with boots and a cute jacket for a look that is always in style.

YARN

Berroco Vintage (#4 medium weight; 52% acrylic, 40% wool, 8% nylon; 218 yd./200 m; 3.5 oz./100 g)
  2 skeins #5175 Fennel

HOOK

U.S. size J-10 (6 mm) crochet hook

GAUGE

3 x 3 box stitches = 2 x 2⅓ in./5 x 5.8 cm

FINISHED MEASUREMENTS

See pattern size table to adjust the size; the skirt length can be adjusted by increasing or decreasing the amount of box stitches.

NOTES

- The design uses the Box Stitch Increase (page 1), Decrease (page 4), Rectangle (page 5), and Box Stitch Join (page 9).

BOX STITCH SIZING—FOREST SKIRT									
	extra sm	sm	med	large	1X	2X	3X	4X	5X
Hips (inches/centimeters)	34 in./ 86 cm	36 in./ 91 cm	40 in./ 100 cm	44 in./ 110 cm	48 in./ 121 cm	53 in./ 134 cm	55 in./ 140 cm	57 in./ 144 cm	62 in./ 156 cm
Hips (number of box stitches)	44	46	52	57	62	68	71	74	80
Length (number of box stitches)	22	23	24	25	26	27	28	28	29

Instructions

Create a box stitch rectangle for your hip size and the desired length and width; the pictured sample is 22 by 44 box stitches, approximately 16 x 34 in./41 x 86 cm. Fold the piece lengthwise in half and join using the box stitch join; do not finish off.

Waistband

Note: Chain 3 counts as the first double crochet on all rounds of the waistband.

Round 1: Take yarn used for the join and slip stich into the first chain-3 opening in the piece. Chain 3 and go around the top of the skirt by working 3 double crochet into each of the remaining chain-3 openings around, join with a slip stitch to beginning chain 3; do not turn.

Round 2: Chain 3, *work 1 double crochet into each of the next 2 double crochet and then double crochet 3 together*; repeat from * to * around the waistband to create the waist decrease, slip stitch to join to beginning chain 3; do not turn.

Round 3: Chain 3, double crochet into each stitch around, join to beginning chain 3 with a slip stitch.

Optional: Make a chain rope to be used as a drawstring to cinch waist if desired or needed. Chain 300 or desired length, turn, slip stitch back into each stitch. Weave loosely through the last round of the waistband and tie closed.

Finishing

Weave in the ends and block.

Raspberry Hat & Fingerless Gloves

This hat and glove set will add a little pop to your winter wardrobe. Choose a bright color like this raspberry to really emphasize the texture. The button on the hat gives a little extra pizazz.

YARN
A & B Fiberworks 100% Alpaca Yarn (#3 light weight; 250 yd./229 m; 3.5 oz./100 g)
> 3 skeins Raspberry

HOOK
U.S. size E-4 (3.5 mm) crochet hook

GAUGE
3 x 3 box stitches = 1¾ x 1¾ in./4.4 x 4.4 cm

FINISHED MEASUREMENTS
Sample hat: circumference 8 in./21 cm
Length including the top closure: 9 in./23cm
Sample gloves, before joining: circumference 9 in./22.9 cm; length 13½ in./34.3 cm

NOTES
- These designs use the Box Stitch Increase (page 1), Decrease (page 4), Beveled Edge (page 7, hat only), and Box Stitch Join (page 9, gloves only).
- Chain 3 counts as the first double crochet of the round.

Hat

Instructions

This hat utilizes the beveled edge to create the part that will wrap around the head. This portion can be adjusted larger or smaller and shorter or taller to fit. You will work the piece so a triangle is created on either end, and the straight portion in between is the part that should fit the circumference of your head, as the triangles will be folded over as a decorative element.

Start by using the box stitch increase until you have a row of 8 box stitches (or desired height of band, keeping in mind that the hat will be closed at the top later). Then use the beveled edge process to work straight until it is 8 by 48 box stitches, or desired circumference not including the initial

triangle. Decrease to create a triangle on the other end, but do not finish off.

Close the Top

Fold the piece so the triangles overlap, as shown in the photos, and use a safety pin or two to hold them in place while you work rounds to form the top of the hat.

Round 1: Attach the yarn into the top right stitch of the beveled edge; chain 3 and 1 double crochet into same space. Work 2 double crochet into the next beveled edge to the left (the other side of the beveled edge at the front of the hat). Continue working around the hat doing 2 double crochet into each beveled edge space, join with slip stitch to the top of beginning chain 3 (40 double crochet); do not turn.

Round 2: Chain 2 (counts as first stitch), work 1 single crochet into next stitch and continue to work 1 single crochet into each of the previous round's stitches; you should have 40 single crochet. Slip stitch into the top of the chain 2; do not turn.

Round 3: Chain 2; work 1 single crochet into each of the next 2 stitches then skip next stitch. For the rest of the row, work 3 single crochet and skip the fourth stitch (30 single crochet). Slip stitch into top of beginning chain 2; do not finish off.

Round 4: Chain 2; work 1 single crochet into next stitch and skip the next stitch. Continue working 2 and skipping the third stitch (20 single crochet). Slip stitch to top of the beginning chain 2; do not finish off.

Round 5: Chain 2; skip next stitch. Continue the row, working 1 single crochet into the next stitch and skipping the second stitch (10 single crochet). Slip stitch to top of the beginning chain 2.

Round 6: Repeat Round 5, decreasing 1 of every 2 stitches (5 single crochet). Slip stitch to top of the beginning chain 2.

Finishing

Tack down the corner of the top triangle and sew a button through both layers of triangles as shown in the photos. Weave in ends and block.

Fingerless Gloves

Instructions

These gloves are easily adjusted to make different sizes. Measure the length between your wrist (or the part of your hand that you want covered) and elbow and around your wrist and middle arm before the elbow. You will want negative ease to hold the gloves on, so keep that in mind when choosing your circumference.

Make two box stitch rectangles (one for each glove) 14 by 22 box stitches (approximately 8 x 12½ in./20 x 32 cm), or desired size; do not finish off.

Joining

Fold each glove in half lengthwise and use the box stitch join to close the glove; do not finish off.

Edging

Once you have closed the length of the glove, continue to work the join process (without joining) along the top edge of the glove to create chain-3 spaces around the top of the glove for the frill; slip stitch to join together.

Round 1: Chain 3, work 9 double crochet into the chain-3 opening, continue by working 10 double crochet into each opening around the glove to make the top frill. Join with slip stitch to first chain 3 and finish off.

Finishing

Weave in the ends and block.

CROCHET STITCH REVIEW

Chain. Yarn over and draw the yarn through to form a new loop.

Slip Stitch. Insert the hook into the work as directed, yarn over and draw through both the work and the loop on the hook.

Single Crochet. Insert the hook into the work as directed, yarn over and draw through the work only, yarn over and draw the yarn through both loops on the hook.

Half Double Crochet. Yarn over and insert the hook into the work as directed, yarn over and draw through the work only, yarn over and draw through all three loops on the hook.

Double Crochet. Yarn over and insert the hook into the work as directed, yarn over and draw through the work only, yarn over and draw through the first two loops only, yarn over and draw through the last two loops on the hook.

Treble Crochet. Yarn over twice and insert the hook into the work as directed, yarn over and draw through the work only, yarn over and draw through the first two loops only, yarn over and draw through the next two loops only, yarn over and draw through the last two loops on the hook.

Triple Treble Crochet. Yarn over four times and insert the hook into the work as directed, yarn over and draw through work only, yarn over and draw through the first two loops on the hook five times.

ACKNOWLEDGMENTS

To my dearest husband, I thank you for all your support and for cheering me on; you're the love of my life.

A special thank you to my dearest friend Gina. I will forever be thankful for those Tuesday morning coffees and pattern writing. Love you lots for your help, your guidance, and most of all your friendship!

As this is my first book, I have to say that my editors have gone above and beyond to help me. I have learned a lot from them, and I truly understand the effort and patience that is required to work with an author and to manage the process of creating this book. Candi and Julie have become my heroes through this process. Thank you both for your patience and teaching.